TOP SECRETS OF REAL ESTATE INVESTMENT

TESTED APPROACH IN ANY TERRITORY

By

Olatunbosun Amao

TABLE OF CONTENTS

INTRODUCTION

"The property boom has made us all feel wealthy, but unfortunately it has lulled many of those nearing retirement into a false sense of security." -Noel Whittaker

There are many persons who are searching for ways to supplement their present income or to replace it altogether. Real estate investing is one of the major ways people seek to do this. It has already been documented that many of the millionaires in the United States made their first million in real estate.

There are many programs and infomercials on television and other forms of media that are promoting various real estate investing programs. They all purport that you can make millions from real estate investing and in that respect they are correct. In spite of the recent problems in the real estate market with subprime loans, the market remains a viable option for investors.

If you are considering real estate investing, then knowledge of the buying, selling, negotiation strategy, and property repairs process will be very important to you. Having an understanding of these processes will save you from losing your money should something not go as planned. You will also have to be aware of the changes in the marketplace. If you know what is required by the make at any given point in time you can surely make some money and prevent major losses.

Possibly the most common kind of real estate investing is flipping. With flipping you buy a home at a very low cost, spend a little money to do some cosmetic repairs and then sell it at a good profit. For flipping to be effective and profitable, you must invest in homes that are located in areas that have high resale value and a buoyant home market. You could find yourself in a financial bind if the home you invested in cannot be sold for over a year.

There is also prime commercial real estate investing. That is investing in things like factories, apartment buildings, commercial space, and hotels. It is possible to make a lot of money on these types of real estate investments. The trick is to locate properties that are going cheap. It is usually easier to find low cost properties in areas that are underdeveloped and are set for an economic boom.

Real estate investing has its own risks and there is no way of being absolutely sure that your investments will even make you a little profit. With this in mind it is important that you do your research on the direction the market is heading in any particular area you are considering investing in. By doing the research, you will be able to make far better decisions about investing.

The real estate investing risks also makes it more difficult, especially at this time in the marketplace, to receive any kind of financing. There are many lenders available for real estate investors but the present climate makes the loan process more challenging. Many, real estate investors, tend to use their own money to pay for the investment and its repairs if needed. If there is a shortfall in funds some will go to friends and family to borrow the money needed.

CHAPTER 1

HOW TO INVEST IN REAL ESTATE - GETTING STARTED

"L and! It's the one thing God isn't makin' any more of!" Truer words have never been said. It will always be possible to pour another widget, but real estate doesn't come that easily. Like anything, you have to be wise about your choices, what you choose to buy and invest in, but if you follow a few simple, basic rules, you'll be onto something that's at least as secure as a passbook savings account, does more for your portfolio, and is often a lot more profitable!

Start by learning how to invest in real estate - What rules? That's simple, too.Buy low, sell high. That's a no-brainer, right? But seriously now.Pick a number. No, not just any number! Pick the number that you can afford to put into a real estate investment and not miss it. That's your target. That's how much you want to look for as your initial investment. If that's five thousand or five hundred, whatever it may be, name it, and then STICK WITH IT. Now comes the hard part.Scour the papers and the Internet. Look for Owner-Finance, for distressed properties, people just is looking to get out of their mortgage with their dignity halfway intact. When people are about to lose a property to the bank, they'll gladly give it to you, rather than see the bank (who they now think of as evil) gaining from their loss. Now remember your figure? That's the MOST you offer on the property, to get it into your name.

But we're not done yet. You'll still have to do what they call Due Diligence. Find out what it's worth on today's market (allowing for how difficult it may be to get sold, get financing, etc.) and make sure that you're not taking on a burden that they were getting out of for good reason. If they're in upside down, (owe more than it's worth,) thank them for their time, wish them good luck, and move on to the next property. No exceptions.

You might get lucky and find the steal of a lifetime the first time you pick up the newspaper. It could happen. More likely, though, you're going to go through a LOT of newspapers and inquiries. That's okay. You're doing your homework, and learning about the market. Soon enough, you won't even have to check. You'll already have a pretty good idea of what the property is worth, because you've been checking the market already.

Getting started in real estate investment - So you got a property? Great! It checks out, and the title and all of that are clear? Fantastic! Shave off costs wherever you can, but don't be dime wise and dollar foolish while you're at it. When you go to rent or resell that property, be sure to be equally diligent, and cover your asset. Make sure that the person's references are good, get enough of a deposit to protect your interests, and rent it for enough that you can set some money aside for repairs, improvements, and hopefully the next one. You're on your way!

WANT TO INVEST IN REAL ESTATE? 7 QUESTIONS YOU MUST ASK YOURSELF BEFORE YOU BUY ANOTHER REAL ESTATE

You've heard that investing in real estate can be very lucrative. Before you get started, here are seven questions to ask yourself.

1. Is this a hobby or a business?

Ask yourself why you want to invest in real estate.
- Do you want another income stream
- Do you want to build equity in a house
- How many sellers and buyers do you want to speak with each day/week/month
- How much time do you have to invest in real estate
- Are you working a full time job
- Are you retired looking for additional income
- What do you want to do with your time?
If you want to build a real estate investing business, then you need to treat it like a business.

Are you going to be a landlord? Then you need to determine how much time you want to spend collecting rent, maintaining the property, making repairs, answering tenant calls late at night, etc.

Or have a property management company handle the tenants and maintenance? Then you need to determine who you will hire to manage your property and how much you will pay them. Typically a property management company will charge one month's rent to locate a tenant and then charge 8%-10% of the monthly rent for collecting the rent and answering all calls from the tenant. You still need to set aside a reserve fund for maintenance.

Maybe you don't want to be a landlord and you want to wholesale property. Then you need to develop a buyer's list of buyers who have the cash to purchase the house. You will still need to work with sellers to locate properties, get it under contract. You then need to get your wholesale buyer to sign the assignment of contract. And you have to make sure you follow up with the closing agent to make sure the deal is funded by the wholesale buyer and the deal closes. You will get your assignment fee once the deal closes.

Here are the questions you need to ask yourself.
- Do you want to be a landlord
- How much time do you want to put into real estate investing
- Do you want to build a business or just make some extra money once in a while

2. Do you want to work directly with sellers?

There are many investors who want to get into the real estate investing business who don't have prior sales experience. Yes, you can call homeowners directly and negotiate the purchase of their home, it is possible. It's even easier when you are speaking with a motivated seller. I mean a seller that is really motivated to sell, not someone who wants to sell, wants full price for their home and just doesn't want to wait for the all cash buyer that will pay retail price.

Are you someone that wants to help these motivated sellers? Do you have it in you to hear their stories over and over? Some of these sellers will break your heart and you will want to help them. You have to make sure that you only work with those that you can help and make a profit for yourself. Just because someone is willing to deed you their house does not mean it is a good deal.

Think about a situation where the seller has two mortgages, judgments, and liens on the property. Yes, you can work this as a short sale and get the liens removed and negotiate with the lender to get a smaller settlement for the payoff of the mortgage. You need to decide if you want to put in the time and effort it takes to negotiate the short sale and get the liens removed. I have seen investors in the short sale negotiation process with the lender for anywhere from 2 months to 18 months. Do you want wait months to close the deal?

You need to decide if you want to work directly with homeowners or have someone handle this for you.

3. Do you want to work directly with buyers?

Once you have a house under contract, it is time for you to find your buyer. The best thing you can do is to build a buyers list before you have a property. Find out where the buyers want to live, then go find a house in that area. It is much easier to find a house for a buyer than it is to find a buyer for a house.

Do you want to take calls from the buyers? They call at all hours, while you are having dinner, before you wake up in the morning, when you are driving to work, etc. Are you willing to drop everything you are doing to take a call from a buyer?

4. Where are you going to get the money?

This is one of the biggest concerns of all real estate investors, where to get the money.

Yes, you can buy a house with little of your own money. Some of the techniques to do this are:
- Buy the house subject-to the existing mortgage
- Have the seller carryback the financing in the form of a note
- Lease/Option the house You can also build relationships with other people who have money, such as
- Private lenders
- Hard Money Lenders
- Mortgage Brokers

The biggest money concern that you never hear about is where to get the money to market your business. You can buy a house sub-ject-to the existing mortgage. But how do you find that house? You have to continue to market, market, market.

Marketing costs money. That is what most of the gurus forget to tell you. You hear all about how you can buy a house with no money down or little money down. What they don't tell you is that you have to spend money on marketing to find the house, and money on marketing to find the buyer.

Before you get started, put together a marketing plan so you know how much money you need to get started.

5. Do you want chunks of cash or cash flow?

What is the reason you want to invest in real estate? Are you interested in getting chunks of cash? Cash Flow? Or Both?

What you want out of real esate investing will help you determine what type of real estate investing you want to get into.

If you are looking for chunks of cash, you have a couple of choices. Consider wholesaling or rehabbing (fix and flip).

If you are looking for cash flow, consider landlording, selling a home with seller financing, or be a private lender.

6. Where do you want to invest?

Many investors will start out in their local market because they are familiar with it and they already have some relationships in the area. It's easiest to start local since you are familiar with house values and have access to local experts to answer your questions.

7. What is your plan to learn more about RE investing?

The most successful real estate investors are those who keep up with the changes in the industry and are constantly learning new techniques.

One of the best things you can do is find a local mentor, some-one who is making money investing in your local market. Ideally, they should be investing in the area that you are interested in. If you want to wholesale properties, find a local investor who is wholesaling properties. Not only will you ask them to mentor you, but they may buy some of your properties from you.

If you are interested in commercial real estate, then you shouldn't spend your time with an investor who deals only with single family homes.

Always continue to learn about Real estate investing. There are many gurus that travel the country teaching real estate investing. Ask the people at your REIA whose products they have purchased and whether or not it helped them in their business.

First determine the niche you want to work to get started. Learn everything you can about that specific niche and create income in that niche before you move on to the next niche. Don't get distracted by the "shiny ball" syndrome.

Real Estate investing can be very lucrative. You need to create a plan, continue to educate yourself, and continue to market for sellers and buyers.

CHAPTER 2

HOW TO INVEST IN REAL ESTATE - TYPES OF OWNERSHIP

With the stock market the way it is these days, people are looking for different places to invest their money and one of those places may just be real estate. I know I know, we came through one of the worst recessions in the history of America that was fueled primarily by a huge bubble in real estate investing.

But the fact of the matter remains that prices on many property investments dropped dramatically because of the recession. Which means that was an excellent time to get into the real estate game.

If you are new to this game, then you have come to the right place because today I want to talk about several different ways of investing in it and I wanted to specifically talk about the different types of ownership that you can come to expect.

How you own your investment is important for a number of reasons including tax purposes, as well as professional liability (what happens if a tenant in your rental house slips and sues you?!). Today I will discuss several ownership entities that you can choose from.

The first type of ownership is simply individual ownership. In this case, all the profits and liabilities flow directly to you as an individual but you are also exposed to the greatest risk.

The next type of ownership is corporate ownership which allows you to limit your liability and also gives you the opportunity to transfer the ownership interest without triggering local transfer taxes in some cases. There are several types of corporations you can form including a C. corporation and an S. corporation. Because an S. corporation allows profits to flow through to you as an individual, many investors prefer this method but check with your accountant and tax lawyer first just to be sure.

The next type of ownership is partnership ownership. If you have several investors going in together to purchase as one, than a partnership may be the right ownership entity for you. Partnerships are usually not treated as separate taxable entities but instead allow everything to flow through to the individual including profit and losses.

Finally, another type of ownership is trust ownership. Many states allow the creation of trusts that operates solely to title these specific types of investments. In this case the trust may not be treated as a taxable entity but as a pass through entity sort of like a partnership. This kind of entity may not be for the average investor as it can be a little more complicated in certain circumstances.

However you choose to own real estate whether as an individual or with your own Corporation or through a partnership or a trust, make sure that the underlying real estate investment is sound, and the potential for profit is large enough to make it a good investment.

BEYOND THE HANDSHAKE - HOW TO INVEST IN REAL ESTATE WITH A PARTNER

Working with one or more partners on a real estate deal is frequently a wise decision, if not a necessity. For beginning investors, taking a partner helps, offset the risk of even a small investment. More experienced real estate investors may want to take on partners for the same reason, since as the deals get bigger, the risk becomes greater. Furthermore, individual investors can often benefit from the wisdom, experience, and diverse perspectives that partners can bring to the table.

But of course, there are pitfalls to the concept of partnership. Many friendships and even familial relations are ruined due to misunderstanding, negligence, incompetence, or just plain bad luck associated with doing business - not to mention the financial impact of partnerships gone wrong. To avoid these dire consequences, you should always have a formal partnership agreement drafted by an attorney, and you should always establish your partnership as an official, legal business entity.

Caution must be taken here. I have had general partnerships with good friends that went really good, but you must be really sure of what you are doing.

A general partnership is established by the simple act of doing business. It does not have to be registered with any governmental body, although it can be formalized with a written agreement. Legally, their is protection for you from the liabilities your partnership creates, which means that your personal assets could come under attack by litigants against your business. Furthermore, your business assets could be seized for actions related to the misdeeds of your partners. In other words, do not operate as a general partnership if you engage in a continuing business relationship with any partners.

To Incorporate or not to Incorporate?

A vastly superior business entity, easily the most popular, is the corporation. By incorporating, you and your partners establish a legally distinct business entity with its own equivalent of a social security number (called an EIN, or "employer identification number"). In fact, a corporation is technically considered a "fictitious person." Thus, unlike a general partnership, a corporation is legally separate from any and all "partners" - or to be more accurate, "shareholders."

There are many advantages to incorporating. Chiefly among them, corporations provide limited liability. Since they are legally distinct, shareholders cannot be held accountable for the actions of the corporation. In other words, if a corporation of which, you're a shareholder issued, your personal assets are safe. Think about it - if you own stock in Wal-Mart, can you lose your house if the company is sued? Of course not. Your losses are limited to your investment. There are some cases in which a shareholder can be held liable in a small corporation, but in many cases you will be protected from liabilities of the business, and, more critical, the misdeeds of your business partners and employees.

Limited Liability Company

The real danger of owning real estate in a corporation is that if one of the shareholders is personally sued for reasons unrelated to the corporation, the creditor may take possession of the debtor's stock certificates. A shareholder's shares are his or her personal property, and thus are at risk. This is why many real estate investors prefer to operate as a limited liability company or "LLC."

An LLC is like partnership in that the business is less formal than a corporation, but it provides liability protection for the owners of the company ("members"). An LLC also provides creditor protection, in that a judgment against one of the LLC owners will not allow a creditor to seize the LLC's asset and potentially ruin an ongoing business.

An LLC does have a federal tax ID number, but it files as a partnership for federal income taxes purposes. For some real estate investors, the partnership taxation model is better than the corporation because of the ability to deduct losses from rental real estate activity.For others, the corporation is better to avoid self-employment taxes on "earned" income from dealer activity, such as flips.

Each investor should consult with a professional tax advisor to determine which is better for his or her own real estate business.

CHAPTER 3

*THE REAL ESTATE INVESTING SECRET REAL
ESTATE INVESTORS DON'T WANT YOU TO
KNOW ABOUT*

As a real estate investor who has managed to attain the Holy Grail of total financial independence I am used to people asking me about the 'secret' to real estate investing. I have had people come up to me in after dinner speeches and ask me to tell them what the formula is, and I have had colleagues in the industry come up and ask me for a secret tip and in each case I have been tempted to take out a ballpoint pen and write at the back of my business card "trust your instincts". That would be being disingenuous as it is just the kind of advice that means everything and nothing.

Let me explain this first. Every investor in the world has to function in a way that is comfortable for them to operate in and that, invariably, requires them to use their instinct when they are going after deals and when they decide to pull out. So to say, that you need to "use your instinct" is just the kind of non-advice that sounds good and means nothing.

So, to cut to the chase, what is the secret of real estate investing? To discuss this here, now, I have to draw on extensive real estate experience that has taken me to different countries. You realise that what I am about to say has been on my mind for some time and I have considered it in some detail and it is part of the advice I give out in my courses, seminars and workshops and it's summed up by two words: "Risk management."

In a sense, any kind of investment is about risk and every kind of investor who wants to be successful tries to manage it successfully in order to come out on top. Real estate is no exception and, if anything, tends to magnify the risks involved which is why risk management becomes so important and the only way to spread the risk in real estate is to have a large number of people contributing to the costs and giving you income as opposed to just a few. This is where multi-family dwellings and apartment blocks come in and this is exactly where an investor's mettle is proved.

Do your homework carefully, pick up the right multi-family dwelling to buy into, arrange to outsource everything so you do not have to deal with tenants yourself (that would definitely is not a good use of your time), use the bulk-buying power of running multiple properties to negotiate tough but fair deals and then get ready to reap the rewards which, as you might have guessed, are considerable.

HOW TO INVEST IN REAL ESTATE WITHOUT USING YOUR OWN MONEY

Real estate investment has gained popularity over in the last five decades. Although this market has numerous opportunities for large profits, owning and purchasing real estate are complex compared to bond and stock investment. It is thus, crucial to learn how to invest in real estate for one to increase their wealth. The following sections describe various forms of real estate investment and what they entail.

Fundamental Rental Properties

This is the oldest form of investment. In this instance, an investor will purchase property and rent it to tenants. The landlord will then be responsible for mortgage payments, taxes and property costs. Ideally, landlords' charges cover this mentioned costs. In other cases, the landlord may charge extra to cover costs until mortgage repayment but, it is strategic to exercise patience and only charge for expenses until the payment of the mortgage. At this time, most of the rent will turn into profit.

Moreover, property will have value appreciation during the mortgage course. In this regard, the landlord's asset will be more valuable. There are some downsides to what may appear like a perfect investment. One can end up with tenants who destroy property or worse, lack tenants in the first place. This leaves one with a negative flow of cash. There is also the issue of locating the correct property. One should choose an area with low vacancy rates besides an area where individuals will prefer to rent. One should note that this form of investment comes with enormous responsibilities.

Real Estate Investment Factions

These resembles mutual funds for leasing properties. For those who wish to own rental properties but do not want the hassles of being landlords, this provides a good solution for them. In this case, a company will purchase or construct a set of condos or apartment blocks and permit investors to purchase them through the corporation, thereby, joining the faction. One investor can own multiple or a single unit but the company running the investment faction manages every unit. In return for management, the company takes a rent percentage. Investment group quality relies wholly on the company providing it. Theoretically it is safe to invest in real estate, but factions are susceptible to similar charges that irk the mutual fund sector. Again, research plays a vital role in knowing how to invest in real estate.

Trading in Real Estate

These traders represent a different breed from the typical purchase-and rent landlords. They purchase properties with the aim of holding them temporarily, frequently for 3-4 months after which they sell the property for profit. This method is also termed flipping properties. It occurs on the basis of purchasing properties that are either considerably undervalued or exist in extremely hot markets.

REITs

These are investment trusts that emerge when corporations use investors' money to operate and buy income properties. People trade and purchase them on the main exchanges similar to other stocks. This form of investment does not include income tax from the corporate whereas, regular companies would incur profit tax during which they would have to allocate profits as dividend should they choose to do so.

Now that you know some of the basic terminology of investing in real estate, you're ready to find out how to do it without you own money.

HOW TO INVEST IN REAL ESTATE WITH ONLY TEN BUCKS

I will show you the easiest way to invest in real estate without investing any money (OK maybe ten bucks) or using any credit. I want to show you how anyone can work from home part time and make money investing in real estate without ever leaving the house.

I will show you how to invest in real estate regardless of the value of the property or the amount owed on the property, just imaging making five thousand or more right away and making a passive income every month. Once again without any money (except maybe the ten bucks) and without using any credit.

Do you have a computer? Do you have internet access? Do you have a phone? If you can answer yes to these three questions, you can be an investor, as a matter of fact you don't even need a phone or internet access. If you have a laptop computer and a Starbucks you are in business. OK, you don't even need a computer, internet access or a phone if you live close to the library.

Nelson Rockefeller one of the richest men in America and the 41st Vice President of the United States said "The secret to success is to own nothing, but control everything. That statement changed my life as it has allowed me to learn that if you own nothing you don't have all the liability and if you control everything you are the one who makes all of the money.

I have perfected a step by step system that will show you what to do today, tomorrow and every day. You will learn where to find properties without spending any money, without driving around and without making a single phone call. There are so many sellers in the market today that want to sell their homes but no one is helping them, sellers who have nice homes, are not late on their payments but just have not been able to sell their home and are looking every day for someone to help them.

You will learn where to find buyers, they will come to you because you will be helping buyers who have not been able to qualify for bank financing or need a second chance and a fresh start.

You are so lucky be investing in today's real estate market, seller's will come to you begging you to buy their homes paying only their payment and a small deposit and they will give you time to pay until you find the buyers who will come to you begging to buy the home with 3%, 5% or more down plus first payment and security deposit. You will pocket the 3%-5% immediately (I require a minimum of 5k down or 3%-5% whichever is greater).

Now you ask why would anyone sell their home to you without any money and without even asking about your credit?

OK, so what is the secret? Are you ready?

There is no secret.

Real estate investors everywhere have been so busy trying to do what is already being done, buying a book or a course of fix and flips, buying properties from auctions and wholesaling the list goes on and on. Here is the bad news 97% of them FAIL and QUIT in the first 90 days.

CHAPTER 4

*EIGHT TIPS FOR LAUNCHING YOUR REAL ES-
TATE INVESTING CAREER*

Everything in this chapter are tools that can be applied to help
anyone get started in real estate investing. I am going to give you
my eight keys to getting started. Let's get started on an amazing
adventure.

The Eight Tips are as follows.

1. Desire
2. Goal Setting
3. Learning What To Do
4. Attending a Real Estate Investing Seminar
5. The Billings Montana Market
6. Finding, a Mentor
7. Your Real Estate Team
8. Just Do IT

1. Desire

Before we get in to the bolts and nails of real estate investing in
I want to talk to you about desire. If you are going to be success-

ful at anything in life including real estate investing you have to have the desire to do it. Desire is defined as longing or craving, as for something that brings satisfaction or enjoyment. Desire stresses the strength of feeling and often implies strong intention or aim. In real estate investing if, you don't have a desire to learn and grow as a human being and get satisfaction out of it, then real estate investing is going to be hard to do. When I go out and look at a property it brings me a lot of joy. Every aspect brings me joy from talking to home owners, figuring out how I can make a deal work, to buying the house and to finding a good homeowner or tenant for the house. Real estate investing may not be for everyone but real estate investing can offer anyone the financial freedom we all crave for. If you do not have the desire for real estate investing that is ok, it can still help you to live your dreams and help you to get where you want to go in the future.

Why is real estate investing an amazing avenue for anyone to live out all of their dreams? Let me ask you a few questions. Do you have enough money to do anything you want? Do you have every-thing you want? No debt? A nice house? Great Marriage? The free-dom to do anything regardless of how much it costs and the time it takes? If you have all of this things then, you are one of the few people in America who does. Most people may be working fifty hours a week and making just enough to pay their bills. In today's day and age, most people are living pay check to pay check, never really knowing if they will make enough to pay the bills that just keep piling up. If you cannot keep up with your monthly bills how are you going to plan for retirement or send your kids to college or have time to enjoy life. The answer to all of these questions is becoming financially free. Now it's not going to be easy everyone will have to get off the couch and out of their com-fort zone. Real estate is proven to be one of the fastest ways to get your out of the rat race of the nine to five and begin living the life you deserve to live. Everyone wants something different out of their life. Some dream of traveling the world, spending more time with family, volunteering, golfing, laying on a beach, giving back to the community, or anything that will make them happy. There are thousands of things that make people happy.

Making it in real estate takes a person who has a strong desire to change their lives for the better and think big. Anyone can become a great real estate investor. It is going to take a lot of work and can be a struggle at times but in the end it will be the most amazing feeling ever. The people that make it in real estate investing all have a few things in common. First, they run their real estate investing business like any other business out there. Second they get out there and network with anyone and everyone.Some people might be like me and have a hard time talking to other people. If you are that is ok, anyone can learn how to become a people person, it just takes hard daily work. You have to push yourself past your comfort zone. The third thing is that you cannot be afraid to fail. Everyone has failed at something but the most successful people out their learn from their failures. The fourth thing is that you have to put a good team together. I will go into putting a team together in a later chapter. The concept of putting a team together is so that when you don't know something you have team members that know what to do and can help you with questions. The can also make sure that you are not working yourself to death. You do not want to be the person doing everything in your business. Doing everything is a receipt for failure. You have to put together good people who you can trust and rely on. The fifth thing is that you need a mentor. Sixth and final is the desire to do it. No one can become successful at something if they don't want to do it and don't get satisfaction out of what they are doing.

2. Setting Goals

Having goals is one of the most important aspects of achieving what you want in life. You don't want to just have your goals up in your head you want to write them down and paste what you have wrote on the wall somewhere or in the bathroom mirror. You want to review your goals daily and read them out loud to yourself. This way you remind yourself everyday why you are building your business.

How should you start to write down you goals? First off you should think big, and by big I mean HUGE. If your goals are too small, you will easily achieve them and have nothing else to look forward too. You should start off by asking yourself the question if I had all the money and time in the world what would I do, what would I buy, how would I spend my time, and how would I spend my energy. Are you starting to write these down? Well, you should be. Think about what you want, spending time with family, traveling the world, the best cars, a castle, owning a small cottage, running for president, having the biggest real estate investment business in your area or in the country. Whatever your dreams and what you want out of your life, write them down. Some of my goals are becoming free, traveling the world, having a Ferrari, having ten vacation homes all over the world. Right now I am just trying to get you out of your comfort zone of thinking and let your imagination run.

There are several ways to set goals. I have learned a lot of ways you can set you goals and there is no right or wrong way. The best ways that I have found to set your goals is to break them up into two categories. First your short term goals. This should be goals from a month out to around a year. The second is your long term goals these goals are you think big goals and what you see for your future.

For year one I like to first make a list of what I want to achieve this year and I will give you an example of how to do that. For year one you want to be very specific first you want to list what you want your income to be at the end of the year, next how much cash in the bank you want (this is money in your checking account, not assets). Next, you want to list how much you are going to give. Giving is a very important, this can be giving to charity, giving of gifts to friends and family, giving to your school or anything you can dream of. As long as what, you give brings joy to others who need it more than you. Next list what bad habits you have that you want to eliminate. Weather is be quitting smoking, spending too much on junk, drinking too much, working too much, not spending enough time with family, too much TV, not exercising and many more. We all have bad habits that need to be changed in order for use to grow as human beings. Under each of these bad practices list out some steps that you can take in order to quit them. If your bad habit is being lazy and not exercising enough, what can you do to change that? Well, you can get a gym membership or a home work out program. Commit yourself you following through with a plan to work out 3-5 days a week. For you to change these bad habits you have to be totally committed and follow through with a detailed plan you set for yourself. After you have your plans in place you should start listing several things you want to achieve or do in the next year. This can be start a successful business, spend time with family, travel to 2-5 places and so on. Now under each of these you should also write a detailed plan on what you need and what you need to do in order to achieve this goals. Finally, you should take all of this information you have a write on page on what you see your life being over the next year. Doing this is a great exercise to really see what you want out of life.

Goals Year One

This is what I am going To Do This Year
Income: $500,000
Cash: $100,000
Give: $20,000

Bad Habits that will be changes:

Over Sleeping 1.Go to bed at 11 p.m. 2. Use a timer and set it for 8 hours 3. Set the timer on the other side of the room

Buying things that you don't need: 1. Going out shopping less 2. If you have the urge to buy something think to yourself is thing item going to help me to achieve my goals of becoming financially free? 3. Tell friends what you are doing, so they can help to stop you.

What I want to Achieve:

Start a successful Real Estate Investing Business: (you should write a detailed step by step plan of everything you need in order to achieve your goal)

Travel: Where do I want to visit? 1. Gators football game (what I need to do it, money, etc)

And last your own page about what you want to achieve using words like I will and only positive words.

For long term goals you don't need to be as specific right now, but you should list them and under them list a few steps or smaller goals that need to be achieved before you are able to achieve them. With the long term goals always think big. Another good exercise for long term goals is to make a collage of you goals. Put pictures of the house you want on it, places you want to travel, a picture of your family, a number of what income you want in or anything you can think of.

3. Learn

Knowledge builds confidence and destroys fear. If you are starting any kind of business, you need to learn the ins and outs of that business first. The best way I have found to learn about real estate investing is to read all about it. But once you know it you have to apply what you have learned. Learning and reading is just one step to take. There are thousands of books on the market about real estate investing and everyone has something you can learn from. You don't just want to read real estate investing books though. You also want to fill yourself with motivational and leadership books. Every successful person that I know if a reader and they all spend at least thirty minutes a day reading something that will teach them about improving their business or helping themselves to become a better person. Some of the best books that I would recommend reading are listed below.

1. Rich Dad Poor Dad by Robert Kiyosaki (read this first and also ready everything in the rick dad poor dad series, great books to start with and will expand you mind)
2. Be a Real Estate Millionaire by Dean Graziosi
3. Flip your way to financial freedom by Preston Ely (this is an E-Book)
4. Four hour workweek by Timothy Ferriss
5. The Attractor Factor
6. Short Sale Pre-foreclosure Investing by Dwan Bent-twyford and Sharon Sestrepo
7. Keys to success, by Napoleon Hill
8. Think and Grow Rich by Napoleon Hill
9. How to win friends and influence people
10. Any Book by John C. Maxwell (he has tons of amazing leadership books)
11. Getting Started in Real Estate Day Trading by Larry Goins
12. The E Myth by Michael Gerber
13. How to be a quick turn real estate millionaire by Ron Legrand
14. The Power of Full Engagement

15. The It Factor
16. Anything by Anthony Robins

There are tons more you can read but these will give you a great start. You should also read books on negotiating, sales, motivation, and biographies on American business people.

I hope this list gives you the knowledge it has given me. If you learn and apply what you have learned from these books there is no reason that you should not become very successful.

4. Attend a Real Estate Investing Seminar

Attending, a Real Estate Investing Seminar, can be one of the best places to learn about real estate investing from some very well known experts. There are several seminars going on all over the country every weekend. If you live in a big city, it will be very easy to find one. If you live in a town like Billings Montana, you might need to travel a little ways to find one. Now most of the best meeting cost money to attend them. Some range from five hundred dollars for three days and some can be up to $20,000. There are a few that I would recommend. Than Merrill is a great speaker to go hear. I have learned a ton from him. You can find his company online by Google searching him. Also, rich dad poor dad has seminars all over the country. I attended one of their seminars in Billings Montana for only $500 dollars and learned a ton from it. There is also Preston Ely, Larry Goins, and hundreds of of speakers out there. If you find a great book that you really enjoyed, then just simple search for that person online and see if they are speaking somewhere or offer a seminar close to you.

Another reason I recommend going to a seminar is because they get you pumped up and motivated. I have not yet found anything else that just gets you feeling like you can do anything. When you get back from one of these seminars you will have tons of energy and knowledge. Every time I get back from one all I want to do is going out and do a deal or ten.

These seminars will also provide you with several opportunities to purchase amazing real estate investing tools, software or learning material at a fraction of the cost. Believe me when I tell you all of the low priced seminars try to sell you something. But a lot of times what they are trying to sell is some really good stuff.

Another reason to attend a seminar is to network with other investors and build relationships with them. You can meet other investors who you can partner with on a deal, sell a deal too, people who will provide you with deals and so on. You should have hundreds of business cards made up and try to give them all out. You never know how much one business card you hand out can make you.

5. Learn About the real estate market in your area

Most real estate investors start their career off my investing around where they live. You can venture out when you have more experience. The reason behind this is because we feel more comfortable with the areas and know the areas better. It is also easier to get local real estate information that we need. Investing in your local market is also cheaper to start out, there is less travel costs, you can see what you are buying and it may give you a feeling a comfort.

First you have to decide which part of town is the best place to invest in. This can be determined by what kind of real estate investing you choose to do. I have not gone over the types of real estate investing but some include rehabbing (fixing up and selling), wholesaling (finding deals and selling them to other investors), buying to rent, and there are a few others. These are the real estate strategies that I use for the most part. When looking at the market, you need to see where other investors are buying their houses. Most of the best deals will be found in low to middle class neighborshoods. By low I don't mean drug infested war zones, what I mean is blue collar safe neighbourhoods that might have somewhat older houses and houses that are not on the higher end price side. Now you can find deals in the higher priced neighbor hoods, but most will be in the low to middle income neighborhoods. When looking where others are buying ask local realtors, other investors or appraisers.

When talking with investors ask them several questions such as what neighborhoods they prefer, what type of houses they buy (3 bed 2 bath), and what they do (rehab, rent, wholesale). You should not look at other investors as competition but try and work with them.

There are different types of markets such as appreciating markets, flat markets, and deprecating markets. Appreciating markets are markets that there is no enough houses or a very high demand for houses which causes the price of houses to go up. The reason there is a high demand for housing can be because of job growth, a very appealing area, or several reason. Flat markets are markets that have no or very little growth. This means that there is not a lot of demand; buy just enough to fill every ones needs. Depreciating markets are where there is a lot more houses than people to fill those houses. This causes house prices to start going down. This can be because of a large employer leaving the area, a natural disaster or just overbuilding. There is an old saying buy in a bust and sell in a boom. In depreciating markets you can pick up several deals, while in appreciating the house prices are going to be much higher and harder to find great deals. The deal will still be out there you just have to know where to find them.

Learning your market is another key to becoming successful. Real estate Brokers and experts in your area can be the best source of information for you. Learn to use them to find out what kind of market you are in. Every market can vary by neighborhood, so make sure you know you market well. I have seen the same houses just one mile apart selling for totally different prices.

6. Find a Mentor

Having a mentor to help you can be your biggest learning experience. Mentors can help you with any questions you may have, walk you step by step through the investing process, give you moral support, you learn from their proven system, and also network you with others in the business. Every successful real estate investor that I know says they owe a lot of their success to the mentors they have and had in their lives. I have had some of the best mentors around me, and I am still learning from them.

When trying to find a mentor I would suggest network with the investors at your local real estate investors club meeting. You can find information about real estate investing clubs in your area by searching for REA or real estate investors club then your area in Google. When you go to the meetings ask around who the biggest investors are. Then ask if you could get together with them sometime and discuss real estate investing. Ask them if they would consider working with you to get their career going offer your services as a bird dog. Bird dogs are people who go out find deals or leads about deals and give them to other investors. A bird dog gets from $500 to $3000 dollars depending on the deal. Make sure that you have a bird dog contract signed with the investors saying that if you find them and deal and they buy it that you get paid a certain amount of money. Being, a bird dog, helps you to build credibility with the investor and they are more likely to mentor you if you have something to offer them.

7. Your Real Estate Team

Building an effective team can make your life as a real estate investor a lot easier. You are only one person and cannot do everything or be an expert in every aspect of real estate investing.Going at a project alone can become one of the most frustrating experiences you will ever encounter. Many people have become frustrated and quite real estate investing because they try and juggle too many things. Make sure that when putting a team together you provide everyone with win-win opportunities. When someone knows that working with you is going to make them money they will put you as a higher priority on their list. But you have to prove it to them that you are the real deal.

People to have on your real estate investing team include

- Real Estate Agents (find the top agent for volume of sales in your area and other agents who work with real estate investors)
- Real Estate appraisers (find an appraiser that has done a few hundred jobs or more and make sure they carry errors and omissions insurance)
- Real estate contractors (good rehab crews that can get the job done in a timely manner, have 3-5 crews and on every deal get 3 estimates done. Ask for referrals from them and make sure they are licensed)
- Real estate attorneys (every investor needs an attorney, they can help to protect your assets, make sure you find one that works with investors)
- A property management company (can manage your properties and will give you leads on property they are managing that might come up for sale)
- Title companies (take care of the legal process and make sure there are no liens against the property you are buying, choose one that does hundreds of closings a year)
- Home inspectors(charge about $400 but will give you a great inspection and could save you thousands

in the long run)
- And your Mentor

These people can help you in various aspects of real estate investing. You might find that there are a couple others that are keys to your business, but this is just a list of a few.

8. Just Do it

There is no better phrase out there then JUST DO IT! Once you have learned all you can networked with investors in Billings and learned real estate investing strategies there is nothing left to do but get your feet wet. There is no better learning tool out there then doing a deal. Once you have completed that first deal you will know what to expect and find out that it is not as hard as you thought it would be. You will have learned what you did right and what was frustrating. Take that experience and ask yourself what would have made it run smoother. Apply that to your next deal.Then the next deal will be easier and it keeps getting easier as you go. I will say that every deal is different from the last, but that what makes this business fun. You have to be creative and always keep on learning and growing with your business.

The average person never uses what they learn. Don't be average apply your knowledge. When going out and doing your first deal act like you have done 1000's of deals. The fastest way to change a habit is to act like it is true.

Five keys for success
1. Specialized Knowledge
2. Tools of a professional
3. Have the mindset of a winner
4. Mentors
5. Money and the knowledge of leveraging it (you don't have to have millions to invest in real estate, there are many strategies

out there to use other people's money, or no money at all)

CHAPTER 5

THINK LIKE A MILLIONAIRE: HOW TO INVEST IN REAL ESTATE

Many people fail to see that skills fade, but assets are forever.

They don't know their entire financial education in their lives is completely WRONG!

Too many people believe that a good job, good skills, and a positive attitude will make them great wealth. The problem is that it just doesn't work that way. People who make an hourly wage and a annual salary cannot build wealth. This is because their money doesn't work for them, and instead they work for their money. This idea keeps them from understanding that the only way to build wealth is to invest in multiple sources of income that you don't have to work for, but instead build yourself or purchase from someone else.

Another misconception of multiple sources of income and passive income is that people assume government and financial institutions offerings such as the stock market, CD's, and many other financial instruments are passive income. Most of the time however, unless it is a note or bond that pays you regular interest. It is not actually passive income or a stream of income. As a stream of income or passive income is income that you make every day, every month, and every year continuously as cashflow. Stocks and the like only make you money on the sale and never anything in the meantime. Meaning they don't ever actually cashflow. For example, it is the same as purchasing a piece of fine art and hoping that it appreciates the longer you hold onto it. Which is risky and locks your money up from better uses.

Real Estate as an Investment

Real Estate is the King when it comes to creating wealth for people. No other offering has the traits and abilities like real estate does. It is constantly appreciating and gaining value. It is always in demand because people need a place to live. And most important of all, it is a real asset that isn't going anywhere soon. Allowing you to borrow against it as collateral and even to write off all expenses and costs associated off on your taxes. Now let's not wait a moment longer to get into Real Estate as an Investment.

Real Estate You Can Buy as Investments

There is so many ways to invest in real estate and the major differences comes to how much capital you will need to put down to purchase them. This could be as little as $40,000 - $50,000 to buy a condo outright, to only $10,000+ to purchase a $100,000 single family home, or to as much as $20,000-$30,000 to purchase a multifamily home (2-4 units). All of which are Residential and can be easily financed.

Once you get past four units, small office buildings, and industrial properties. You're going into commercial territory and have a lot more hoops to jump through as well as have to start working with commercial lending which can require sizable amounts of capital before they will lend. In the rear, is my personal favorite of mobile homes and parks. Which are hard to sell, but can cashflow in all sorts of amazing ways from lending on the mobiles themselves to charging them for renting the use of the land. All of which is taxed as land which is the cheapest tax rate you can have on property.

· Condos/Flats - Condos and flats are some of the best to buy for cashflow as they give the best cap rates. The only issue comes on the resale as many can be hard to finance as an investment property, preventing a large portion of the population from being able to purchase them.

· Single-Family Homes - Single-family homes are easy to rent, easy to sell, and easy to finance.

· Duplexes/Triplexes/Quads - Small multifamily properties (2-4 units). These property types combine the financing and easy purchasing benefits of a single-family home with the cashflow benefits and less competition found in larger investments.

· Small Apartments - Small apartment buildings are made up of between 5-50 units, they can make great cashflow, but can be very illiquid on the resale.

· Small Commercial Office Space - Buying small commercial buildings and renting out office space to business professionals.

· Industrial Properties- Manufacturing, warehouses, distribution centers, etc.

· Mobile Homes - Inexpensive way to enter the world of real estate investing and can also experience significant cashflow.

· Mobile Home Parks - The entire park in which mobile homes are situated on can also be bought and sold. Rent the individual lots to mobile home owners, and as well as having corporately owned and leased ones.

Strategies in Finding Investment Properties

Just as there are a million ways to skin a cat; there is a million ways to find properties for investment. Of the many ways to find the properties for investment. The most common ways are to find the owner directly and give them a cash offer, to find properties that are owned by a lender or bank that they want to get rid of at a discount, or purchase a lien on the property so you can foreclose on the property yourself.

Lease Options - Buying the property and "renting" it with the legal right to buy it later.

For Sale By Owners (FSBO) - Private owners sell their property themselves with a sign or newspaper advertisement, they may want to sell their properties at a discount to avoid paying a realtor.

REO's - Foreclosed Property owned by banks can be bought under market if the demand isn't too high

Auction at the Courthouse Steps - During the process of foreclosure, a home is brought to the courthouse steps to be sold to the highest bidder.

Buying in Pre-foreclosure - Sellers on the brink of losing their home can be very motivated to sell their home and save their credit and their lives.

Short Sales - A bank will often take less than the loan amount on a property to save from the hassle and costs of foreclosing and reselling.

Tax Liens - When homeowner's refuse to pay their taxes, the

government can foreclose and resell the property.

HUD Foreclosures - When a US government ensured loan is foreclosed on, it often becomes the property of the department of Housing and Urban Development.

VA Foreclosures - Similar to the HUD foreclosures, the US Department of Veteran's Affairs sells their homes as well after foreclosing on one of their insured properties
Strategies in Buying, Renting, and Selling Properties:

When you finally have the property in your grasp, there are many techniques you can use to maximize your return. Some properties are great for buy n' holding. Meaning you buy them for cashflow, but are expecting to also make a sizable return on the resale due to appreciation. Next up is Fixing N' Flip/Hold, which is finding properties undervalue and fixing them up to either hold onto for cashflow or to sell immediately for instant profit. Then there is Turn-key-Investing, this is where you find the property, turn it into a profitable cashflow and sell it as a source of income to a big fish investor. For Big Commercial, there is NNN leasing that entails having the company renting the property takes care of all the trimmings of the property and pays you for leasing the space. Another Buy N' Hold strategy that can make decent money is to turn your Buy N' Hold property into a Vacation Rental and charge 3x as much than a normal lease. Then there is hard money lending, where you finance others in their fix n' flips, buy n' holds, or primary residence.

Buy-N-Hold - Buy real estate, rent it, and hold it until the market is up and a great buyer comes along.

Fix-N-Hold- Buy below market value, remodel to force appreciation, and held until the market improves and sell it

Fix-N-Flip - Buy well below market value, remodel to market prices, and sell it immediately to get your return.

Turn-Key-Investing - fix-and-flipper, but sells remodeled properties to out-of-town individuals seeking a good place to keep their money moving.

NNN Lease - Big Businesses rent the building and pay all costs associated with the building such as maintenance, taxes, insurance, and more. We can own these buildings for highly-passive income.

Vacation Rentals - Buying vacation property and renting it out off and on season (Snowbirds)

Cash Purchase, Sell on Contract - Buy properties and immediately re-sell them to buyers who may not be able to conventionally qualify for a mortgage. Collect a large down payment when using this method.
How to Finance:

Financing is readily available to anyone who has a cash for a down payment. Below is the major ways you can finance your Real Estate Investments.

All Cash - Property with no mortgage attached is very stable and a safe return. May not be as great as when using leverage (like a mortgage)

Seller Financing - Seller owns a property free-and-clear (no mortgage), and can be negotiated with to find a finance deal

Unconventional Lending - There are many lenders who will lend on any deal you have as long as the number make sense, this can be anything from landlord loans, had money, and much more

Self-Directed IRA - If you have a 401(k), throw it out, it's time to put that money in a self-directed IRA and make that money finally work for you than expecting some money manager who is just trying not to lose your money than make you any. You can use your money in your SD-IRA to do all the strategies in buying, selling, and renting.

20%-25% Down Conventional Investment Mortgage - buy a real estate investment through a bank. Come up with 20-25% down payment and have the bank finance the rest

10% HomePath Investment Mortgage- These loan types are only available on Fannie-Mae backed bank REOs, but can allow an investor to purchase the home for just 10% down payment with other benefits.

Home Equity Line of Credit (HELOC) - With significant equity in real estate, M&T can borrow a line of credit off M&T Real Estate equity.

Small Business Loans - Banks often will finance a line of credit or loan for small businesses- to include a real estate investment company

If you have the mind for real estate or want to hire someone who does, then you should forego a large portion of your portfolio to invest in real estate. It easily as one of the highest returns than any other investment in the world, the only caveat, like anything else, is that you need to do it right to be successful.

CHAPTER 6

HOW TO INVEST IN REAL ESTATE DURING
ECONOMIC DEPRESSION

If history is of any value to us, then looking at past recessions and depressions shows that during such periods of time real estate value diminishes. This is because of tight credit - during rough economic times credit is scarce and interest rates are high - only very small percentage of people and only economically sound business proposals do get credit.

There are more sound investment areas during economic depressions: precious metals, food and energy - the essentials. One might argue that precious metals are not the essentials, but humans use them as preservation storage of wealth (especially when there is a hyperinflation possibility on the horizon), thus it is essential. But if you are bent on investing in real estate - read on.

Depression can be inflationary or deflationary. In 1930 depression in US was deflationary - the prices of goods and services went down and money was scarce. In such environment real estate loses value as there are few buyers - mostly bargain hunters - prudent individuals and businesses who saved money during boom time and now buy real estate for investment, income generation or for business development. Residential, real estate prices, go down depending on the area - less prestigious or further away it is from major centers of employment -the bigger the price drop.

A few years back, the world was in a depression state - prices of goods and services were dropping due to weak demand. Low interest rates were supposed to encourage new house purchases and jump start the real estate market, but because consumers were buried in debt from past excesses and were trying to pay it off, there were very few of them on the market for new houses.

Governments in most developed countries were bankrupt and could not possibly repay the huge amounts of debt they accumulated in the past years. There were only two possible outcomes: bankruptcy or massive currency devaluation. Currency devaluation was out of the question because all the governments were trying to devaluate their respective currencies right to become more competitive and what happens when everybody tries to pull the blanket their own way - it either balances out or the blanket gets torn apart.

Bankruptcy of one of the big countries will have a domino effect and it will lead to the bankruptcy of the world monetary system. Economic expansion in the last 50 years was fueled by credit; and money printing worked in the past bubbles because they were relatively small, but bubbles grew bigger and bigger each time and now we have a systemic crisis - a mother bubble. Who will lend money to the lenders? - Printing presses - the vicious circle which will lead to hyperinflation and ultimately to the bankruptcy and emergence of new monetary system backed by precious metals. Hyperinflationary environment is not good for real estate investment either - the prices lag way behind inflation pace.

What is real estate investor to do during such bad times?

First, what not to do: Do not use any credit unless you get a low fixed interest rate for the duration of the loan and no inflationary adjustments on principal (dream on on getting that!). Well, truth to be told, you never know, you might find some desperado willing to lend on such terms.

Second, invest for value:

- If you buy a residential property, the property better have good tenants living in already; who have been there for a while. Avoid ghost towns - areas where more than 20% of houses are for rent or for sale. If property is not rented, check around the neighborhood for asking renting prices and subtract 25% from that - this will be the price you realistically will be able to rent for. I find good value in buying a rundown property, giving it a nice facelift on a budget and getting more rental income because of that.

- If you buy a commercial property with renting it in mind - the same rules as above apply. I would like to add one thing- if it is a storefront - it better be located in an area with high pedestrian traffic. I will not touch office space right now with a mile long post. That bubble is yet to burst!

- If you plan to buy an income property - a parking lot, a producing farm, reforestation project, etc. - do your DUE diligence - don't trust sellers on anything - you never know what pressures are on them to sell! I have seen business owners faking income statements in a desperate attempt to get rid of a bad business. Go to the bank to check their statements - if seller refuses any reasonable financial check - down walk away - run away.

HOW TO INVEST IN REAL ESTATE WITH YOUR SELF-DIRECTED IRA

What is a Self-directed IRA?

Unlike a regular IRA that you open with a brokerage firm, a self-directed IRA lets you take control of your own investment. And you're not limited to only stocks, bonds and mutual funds.

What can you invest in with a self-directed IRA?

With a self-directed IRA, you can invest in real estate, private equity, promissory notes or mortgage notes, foreign currencies, offshore funds, commodities, such as oil or petroleum and precious metals, such as gold, silver, etc.

How to use a Self-directed ROTH IRA in your real estate investing?

If you contribute money to your Roth IRA, that money grows tax-free, since your contributions are after-tax money. With what you have in a self-directed Roth IRA, you can purchase rental properties. The rental income that is generated is tax-free. When you sells your rental property for a profit, it is tax-free. If you ever ended up in legal litigation, your real estate properties in your self-directed IRA is protected, because you don't own it. Your IRA owns the properties.

Isn't that a great retirement plan and asset protection strategy?

How do you buy real estate properties with a self-directed Roth IRA?

First of all, you need to have a self-directed Roth IRA account set up. You can purchase real properties in one of several ways. If you have enough money in your IRA, you can purchase with all cash. Another option is to purchase with a non-recourse loan, which requires at least 50% of purchase price as a down payment. One thing to remember is that non-recourse loan carries higher interest rates, which may eat into your profit or cash flow.

So my suggestion is, if your fund in your IRA is not enough to purchase a real property all cash, then consider other investment options to build up your cash first.

You may build up your cash by lending money through companies like Prosper.com. Prosper.com and some other organizations allow you to open a self-directed IRA to fund your lending business.

Or you can invest in other types of investment offer through your IRA company.

Either way, a self-directed is a great way to diverse your retirement investment and gives you more control. Some self-directed IRA companies even give you "check-book control," which means you have to ability to write checks out whenever you need the money, instead of making a request from the company and waiting for the checks.

HOW TO INVEST IN REAL ESTATE OUTSIDE YOUR AREA WITH EASE

Many people are going outside of their own market to purchase quality real estate investments at a fraction of the price. Did you know that for example a $400,000-$500,000 home in California is similar to an $80,000 home in Dallas, Little Rock, or Memphis? Did you know that the rent on a home that price can be as high as $1000 per month or more?

Your peers are buying properties in these other markets, getting a lot of cash flow for their money and are racking up a diverse portfolio of assets quickly. Are they geniuses? Are they better real estate investors? The answer is no. Many of these people stepped outside their comfort zone, took very little risk, and now are reaping the rewards. How are they doing this? Let's take a look.

1. Taking advantage of Markets - First, real estate investors in markets that had a large run up in prices in many cases are hurting now that the appreciation is gone. The savvy investors from these markets are looking outside and they are looking for positive cash flow. Many markets in the interior of the US, especially the South, are not only growing markets but have had depressed prices for quite some time. This is a better angle to look at then for example a rust belt city in the Midwest with a declining population and factories closing up. Look where the economic growth is and the prices have been low. Example: Memphis, Dallas, Little Rock, Atlanta, Birmingham, Montgomery, and others.

2. Do your homework - Look online and find local Real Estate Investing Associations. Try http://www.nationalreia.com and look for associations in your target market. See if you can access the forums section of their websites. Who are the movers and shakers? Who is buying and selling a lot of property? Then look at other sites such as Craigslist in the same market. Do you see any correlation? You should see some repeat names, similar deals, etc.Use this information to start evaluating homes.Next, use Google, Yahoo, MSN, others. For example: if you Google the following, what companies surface: sample city, real estate investing, or sample city discount properties. Look for reputable companies that are selling properties. If they don't have an established website, stay away. Typically people that are one man shows don't have a good support staff.

3. Interview to build a real estate investing team - After searching on line and finding out who is buying and selling a lot of property, make a list and interview them. Find out who their support staff is.Does this buyer and seller work specifically with rehab crews? How about management companies?Closing Attorneys or

Escrow Agents? You should interview three of each of these or more. Be brutally honest. If you can tap the wisdom of a team, the process of owning property outside your area can be easy. Make sure the management companies are willing to work with the real estate investment contractors, the sellers of your property, and so on. Ask about the reputations of each to the others.

4. Book a Flight - Make a trip to your new market to meet your team, go out into the streets, look at available property, and see everyone's office. This will often be the true test. It is easy to create a false online front, or a front over the phone, but very difficult to cover up after you show up at their doorstep. Spend 2-3 days in your market. Look at all the neighborhoods the wholesalers or agents work in. Make sure they aren't going to sell you war zones. Ask them about the rent ranges, rehab estimates, time to rent, etc. Verify this numbers with the management companies and contractors. If all checks out, proceed. The right team of people will come to light.

5. Buy and start slowly. Many people will try to push you to purchase several properties at one time. By a property or, 2 within your risk threshold and see how it performs if it performs well: wash, rinse, and repeat. You've uncovered a new real estate investing market! Hopefully you had a little fun and explored a new area too.

HOW TO MAKE $2 MILLION AND $90,000 PER YEAR INVESTING IN REAL ESTATE

More millionaires made their fortune investing in real estate that in any other profession. In today depressed housing market it is possible for the ordinary investor to make his or her millions by investing in real estate - but only if you do it correctly.

Many potential real estate investors jumped into the market five years ago with the expectation of buying a property, fixing it up and then selling it for a profit. This was an easy strategy to follow since home prices were appreciating up to 100% a year in several areas of the United States. Outside these super hot areas, it was not unusual to see home prices soar 20 percent annually in most other areas of the country. It is easy to make millions in a market where prices are increasing at these rates. The crash of the housing market in 2006 effectively ended this strategy of making millions in real estate.

There was a period housing prices declined on average 32 percent throughout the united states. There was an abundance of properties that were selling for a mere 20-50 percent of their market value. Buying these properties is following the popular investing adage of "buy low and sell high." My suggestion is to modify this adage to read "buy low, rent for 5-10 years for positive cash flow and then sell high." This is the best strategy to follow in our current housing market.

Let me give you an example of how this strategy works. A house that sold for $100,000 in 2005 was listed for sale for $40,000. Most mortgage companies require you to put down 25% of the purchase price and will finance the balance. This requires you to put down $10,000 to purchase this house and you get a 10-year mortgage for $35,000. If you get an interest rate of 6%, your monthly payments would be $388.57. You spends an additional $5,000 rehabbing the property in order to get it rent ready.

Now you are ready to start making your millions and here is your strategy. This process will involve investing for 10 years and then not investing for the next ten years. After 20 years you will have properties with a value of over $2 million and you will be collecting $7,500 per month in rents.

You rent the property for 10 years at a monthly rental rate of

$750. Even with insurance and taxes, you should be clearing a positive cash flow of $200 per month. Over the 10 year period that is a $24,000 profit. In ten years the housing market should have recovered and you will be able to sell the house for $100,000. Since your mortgage has been paid off, you have made a $100,000 profit on the sale. Total profit is $124,000 on your initial $15,000 investment. That $124,000 profit is a far cry from making millions. The strategy involves buying one house a year for those ten years.

After 10 years you will have 10 properties. For the next 10 years you sit back and continue to rent the 10 properties that you have. At the end of that 10 years all of your mortgages will be paid off. At this point, you will be collecting $7,500 per month. This revenue stream will continue for decades and decades. Your properties will probably be worth $200,000 each or a combined total of $2 million.

For that 10 years you have invested $150,000 on the purchase of the 10 properties. That investment resulted in an income stream of $90,000 per year and property worth $2 million. This is why you buy and hold real estate in a down market.

CONCLUSION

MYTHS ABOUT INVESTING IN REAL ESTATE

Investing can be done in more ways than one. Those unaware on the ways of how to invest in real estate, say it is difficult to invest and make money out of it and that is a myth. It is a matter of knowing what you have, don't have and can have. You may not have the money but you may have good contacts, good business sense and foresight, and the time. With this, you can have real estate. Research and news updates about future land needs are important tools. Don't imagine big time because you could also lose big time. Look at remote properties that are dirt cheap but have good potentials within 2 to 5 years. The important attitude here is not to be in a hurry. The meager amount you'll be putting in can be considered as part of your forced savings. Land values will appreciate and so with your money in the land.

It will take time for real estate to recover and money will be tied up to it. There are states or locations where business would recover faster. This is based on employment, commerce and federal programs geared towards development. The trends of these factors usually affect real estate movements. The myth becomes true only when investment is made in locations that do not have the necessary business pace. Wild speculation on a locations' development might also make the myth plausible. Many types of investments take time to realize good profits or gains and are also dependent on the flow of trade and commerce. The best protection in investment is that the land will not vanish or get lost. Over time, compared to other investments, values will definitely go up. This is actually a myth that's worth it in time.

Real estate investment has too many ins and outs and involves a lot of money. The ins and outs are in truth, options on what you can do. It is like different specializations in the business. You can just hold it, flip it, develop it or use it as collateral if you have other business that needs additional funds. A lot of money will depend on the real estate investment that you want to get into. Talking about prime real estate then you'll really need a deep pocket. On developing land, it could always be done through joint venture or partnership! In this manner, the partner is the one who shells out the money for development. As long as contracts and sharing agreements are in order, there will be no issue to worry about. There is also no problem in marketing because once a real estate project is completed; many realty out-fits will offer their services on commission basis. Development and marketing are ins and outs involving money an investor does not really have to be concerned of. This only becomes a myth to those who only look at real estate investment on its face value and not on all the opportunities contained in it.